HOLDING SPACE FOR YOURSELF

60-day journal prompts for innerpeace

Make yourself a priority.

Create habits that take care of your mental, emotional and spiritual wellbeing.

HOLDING SPACE FOR YOURSELF
Copyright @2023 by Lois Goudeau
60-day journal prompts for innerpeace

Paperback ISBN: 979-8-9911150-5-6

Gentle Rain Publishing
gentlerainpub@gmail.com

Day 1

Setting Intentions

MORNING

Today, set a powerful intention for this 60-day journey.

Write down your commitment to nurturing your mental health and overcoming workplace stress.

How will you embrace this challenge?

_____

_____

_____

_____

_____

_____

_____

Day 1

EVENING

Now, as the day comes to a close, set your sights on tomorrow.

How will you carry forward this commitment?

Write down one action you'll embrace to support your well-being and face the challenges.

_____

_____

_____

_____

_____

_____

_____

Day 1

Day 2

Morning Moments

MORNING

Describe your morning routine and how you can connect it with mindful moments.

Share the sensations, thoughts, and emotions that arise as you create a peaceful morning.

_____

_____

_____

_____

_____

_____

_____

Day 2

EVENING

As we end another day, take a moment to reflect on how the day unfolded.

Write about the experiences, the challenges and the emotions. Remember every experience, whether triumphant or trying, holds a lesson and an opportunity for growth.

_____

_____

_____

_____

_____

_____

_____

_____

Day 2

Day 3

Gratitude Attitude

MORNING

Write about three things you're grateful for today.

Dive deep into the feelings these blessings reveal and how practicing gratitude shifts your perspective.

Day 3

EVENING

Write about how cultivating gratitude has helped you navigate the challenges of the day, allowing you to release stress and embrace a more balanced, empowered mindset.

_____

_____

_____

_____

_____

_____

_____

Day 3

Day 4

Creative Bliss

MORNING

Engage in a creative activity today, whether it is painting, writing, crafting, or any form of artistic expression.

How will you approach this activity?

_____

_____

_____

_____

_____

_____

_____

Day 4

EVENING

Share your experience of
engaging in the creative activity.

How did it make you feel?

Did it help you disconnect from
workplace stress?

If so, how?

_____

_____

_____

_____

_____

_____

_____

Day 4

Day 5

Digital Self-Care

MORNING

Rearrange your digital space. Write down what this will look like.

Unfollow negative accounts and fill your feed with positivity and inspiration.

Your online world should be a reflection of your well-being.

_____

_____

_____

_____

_____

_____

_____

Day 5

EVENING

Describe your digital detox experience.

How did unplugging from negativity impact your mood and energy?

What insights did you gain about your stress level?

_____

_____

_____

_____

_____

_____

_____

Day 5

Day 6

Nature's Embrace

MORNING

Make a commitment to immerse yourself in nature.

Whether it's a walk in the park, a hike, or simply sitting under a tree, how do you think the healing power of nature will rejuvenate your spirit and reduce stress?

_____

_____

_____

_____

_____

_____

_____

Day 6

EVENING

Write about your nature connection today.

Share details of the outdoor space you visited and how the sights, sounds, and smells affected your state of mind and stress level.

Day 6

Day 7

Breath By Breath

MORNING

Pause and take five minutes to focus on your breathing.

Inhale deeply, exhale slowly.

What stress do you feel melting away as you bring your attention to the present moment?

Repeat your breathing throughout the day.

Day 7

EVENING

Reflect on your mindful breathing practice.

How did it help you center yourself throughout the day?

Write about moments when you tuned in to your breathing and found calm in the middle of chaos.

_____

_____

_____

_____

_____

_____

_____

Day 7

Day 8

Spreading Joy

MORNING

Spread some love!

Perform a random act of kindness today.

It could be a smile, a compliment, or lending a helping hand.

How do you think this will improve your mood and reduce stress?

_____

_____

_____

_____

_____

_____

_____

Day 8

EVENING

Describe the act of kindness
you shared today.

How did it feel to uplift
someone else's spirits?

What are some of the mental
or emotional benefits you
experienced?

_____

_____

_____

_____

_____

_____

_____

Day 8

Day 9

Connect With
Loved Ones

MORNING

Reach out to a friend or family member who uplifts you.

How will sharing laughter, stories, and moments of connection remind you of the support you have?

_____

_____

_____

_____

_____

_____

_____

Day 9

EVENING

Did you share laughter, stories, and moments of connection?

How did those moments help reduce workplace stress and improve your self-esteem?

_____

_____

_____

_____

_____

_____

_____

Day 9

Day 10

Mindful Nourishment

MORNING

Create a savory meal today with the intention of reducing stress.

During one meal, practice mindful eating.

Fully engage your senses as you savor the meal. Describe the flavors, textures, and sensations of each bite.

_____

_____

_____

_____

_____

_____

_____

Day 10

EVENING

Write about the meal you savored mindfully today.

How does this mindful experience contribute to your overall sense of calm and well-being?

_____

_____

_____

_____

_____

_____

_____

Day 11

Restful Thoughts

MORNING

Create a bedtime ritual to promote better sleep.

What will you do?

Dim the lights?

Read a calming book?

Or disconnect from screens at least an hour before bed?

Create this routine.

_____

_____

_____

_____

_____

_____

_____

Day 11

EVENING or NEXT MORNING

Detail your bedtime ritual and how it contributed to your quality of sleep.

How did winding down with intention affect your dreams and morning energy?

_____

_____

_____

_____

_____

_____

_____

Day 11

Day 12

Reflection Time

MORNING

Set aside time to reflect on your journey
so far.

What practices have resonated with you?

How are you feeling?

_____

_____

_____

_____

_____

_____

_____

Day 12

EVENING

What insights have you gained about workplace stress and mental health?

_____

_____

_____

_____

_____

_____

_____

Day 12

Day 13

Letting Go and
Lightening Up

MORNING

Release what no longer serves you.

Declutter a space in your home, donate unused items, and make room for positive energy to flow.

How did this impact your mood?

_____

_____

_____

_____

_____

_____

_____

Day 13

EVENING

Describe the decluttering process you engaged in today.

How did releasing physical clutter create space for mental clarity and emotional release?

_____

_____

_____

_____

_____

_____

_____

Day 13

Day 14

Envisioning Balance

MORNING

Close your eyes and visualize your ideal, stress-free workday.

What do you see?

_____

_____

_____

_____

_____

_____

_____

Day 14

EVENING

Write about your visualization exercise.

How did visualizing a stress-free workday
help shift your mindset and inspire
actions toward achieving that vision?

_____

_____

_____

_____

_____

_____

_____

Day 14

Day 15

Self-Love Celebration

MORNING

Celebrate your journey so far!

Reflect on the transformations you've experienced throughout these 15 days!

_____

_____

_____

_____

_____

_____

_____

Day 15

EVENING

You've prioritized your mental health.

Treat yourself to a soothing bath, a favorite meal, or simply bask in the feeling of accomplishment.

Describe how you pampered yourself.

Day 15

Day 16

Inner Reflection

MORNING

Write about the changes you've noticed in your thoughts, emotions, and actions.

_____

_____

_____

_____

_____

_____

_____

Day 16

EVENING

How have your daily practices shaped
your mindset and overall well-being?

_____

_____

_____

_____

_____

_____

_____

Day 16

Day 17

Setting Boundaries

MORNING

Today set healthy boundaries to protect your time.

What will that look like?

_____

_____

_____

_____

_____

_____

_____

Day 17

EVENING

Describe the healthy boundaries you established today.

How did setting limits and protecting your time contribute to your mental well-being and reduce workplace stress?

_____

_____

_____

_____

_____

_____

_____

Day 17

Day 18

Movement and Mindfulness

MORNING

Today, combine mental and physical well-being.

Complete a movement with mindfulness, whether it's yoga, stretching, or a mindful walk.

Write about how you're going to complete this activity.

_____

_____

_____

_____

_____

_____

_____

Day 18

EVENING

Write about your experience combining movement with mindfulness.

How did connecting your body and mind enhance your sense of balance?

_____

_____

_____

_____

_____

_____

_____

Day 18

Day 19

Joyful Ritual

MORNING

Review your daily morning ritual.

Think about how you can add more joy into this routine.

Detail the joyful ritual you will incorporate into your day.

_____

_____

_____

_____

_____

_____

_____

Day 19

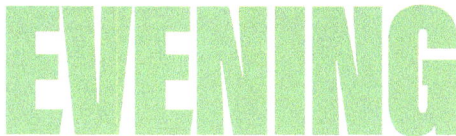

EVENING

How did this ritual bring a sense of delight and playfulness to your routine, helping you combat workplace stress?

_____

_____

_____

_____

_____

_____

_____

Day 19

Day 20

Reconnect With
Passion

MORNING

Is there a hobby or passion that you've stop doing?

Write how you will rekindle that passion or hobby today.

_____

_____

_____

_____

_____

_____

_____

Day 20

EVENING

How did immersing yourself in something you love ignite your spirit and help you let go of work-related stressors?

_____

_____

_____

_____

_____

_____

_____

Day 20

Day 21

Affirming Self-Love

MORNING

Write down 3 positive affirmations that can help with anxiety or stress.

Repeat them throughout the day.

Day 21

EVENING

Write about the affirmations you repeated today.

How did these positive declarations of self-love and empowerment uplift your spirit and reduce workplace stress?

_____

_____

_____

_____

_____

_____

_____

Day 21

Day 22

Cultivating Patience

MORNING

Practice patience today.

Choose to focus on progress instead of perfection.

What are some ways you can be patient with yourself?

_____

_____

_____

_____

_____

_____

_____

Day 22

EVENING

Reflect on moments when you practiced patience today.

How did embracing patience shift your perspective and help you navigate workplace stressful situations?

_____

_____

_____

_____

_____

_____

_____

Day 22

Day 23

Mindful
Communication

MORNING

Practice mindful communication today.

Paying attention is one of the most important aspects of mindful communication.

What are ways you can apply mindful communication today?

_____

_____

_____

_____

_____

_____

_____

Day 23

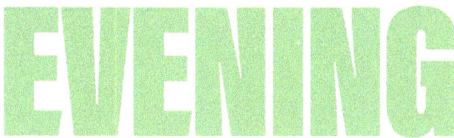
EVENING

Describe your experience of practicing mindful communication.

How did active listening and thoughtful responses improve your interactions and foster a sense of connection?

_____

_____

_____

_____

_____

_____

_____

Day 23

Day 24

Tech-Free Time

MORNING

During the day, create tech-free moments.

How will this look?

_____

_____

_____

_____

_____

_____

_____

Day 24

EVENING

Write about your tech-free moments today.

How did disconnecting from screens allow you to be present, engage with your surroundings, and foster a sense of calm?

_____

_____

_____

_____

_____

_____

_____

Day 24

Day 25

Nature Immersion

MORNING

Create a time to take in nature.

Whether it's a walk, picnic, or simply spending time outdoors, how will you connect with nature?

_____

_____

_____

_____

_____

_____

_____

Day 25

EVENING

Share your day's nature experience.

How did nature's embrace rejuvenate
your spirit and provide peace from
workplace stress?

_____

_____

_____

_____

_____

_____

_____

Day 25

Day 26

Culivating Resilience

MORNING

Resilience in action involves being able to regulate emotions during times of stress.

What strategies will you use to maintain your peace?

_____

_____

_____

_____

_____

_____

_____

Day 26

EVENING

Reflect on challenges you faced today.

How did you tap into your resilience and coping skills to navigate these challenges while prioritizing your mental well-being?

_____

_____

_____

_____

_____

_____

_____

Day 26

Day 27

Giving Grace

MORNING

Practice self-compassion for
yourself and others today.

It may feel forced at first but think
about the ways you can extend
this grace.

Write it down.

_____

_____

_____

_____

_____

_____

_____

Day 27

EVENING

Describe how you extended grace to yourself and others today.

How did these gestures of compassion enhance your sense of fulfillment and contribute to reduction in workpace stress and your well-being?

_____

_____

_____

_____

_____

_____

_____

Day 27

Day 28

Mindful Time Management

MORNING

Managing your time better can reduce your likelihood of experiencing burnout.

Write down 3 mental techniques to improve your time management.

Ex- make a plan, break down tasks, or start early.

_____

_____

_____

_____

_____

_____

_____

Day 28

EVENING

Write about your approach to time management today.

How did mindful planning and prioritization alleviate workplace stress and help you focus on what truly matters?

_____

_____

_____

_____

_____

_____

_____

Day 28

Day 29

Rethink It

MORNING

Today, practice reframing your perspective so you can find the silver lining in any situation.

Write about how this will empower you to deal with the day's challenges.

_____

_____

_____

_____

_____

_____

_____

Day 29

EVENING

Share a situation where you turned a potentially negative experience into a moment of gratitude.

How did reframing your perspective decrease workplace stress?

_____

_____

_____

_____

_____

_____

_____

Day 29

Day 30

Reflection and Renewal

MORNING

Take a moment to reflect on the first 30 days of this journey.

How have your daily practices shaped your mindset and overall well-being?

_____

_____

_____

_____

_____

_____

_____

Day 30

EVENING

Write a letter to yourself
acknowledging your commitment
to your mental well-being.

Day 30

Day 31

Reflection and Progress

MORNING

Continue to reflect on your growth over the past month.

Write about the changes you've observed.

_____

_____

_____

_____

_____

_____

_____

Day 31

EVENING

As you reflect on the changes you wrote about this morning, did you carry forward any of them during the course of the day?

If so, which ones?

_____

_____

_____

_____

_____

_____

_____

Day 31

Day 32

Mindful Moments

MORNING

Being present and aware is a key feature of mindfulness. It increases stress resilience and effective coping.

What ways can you be present today?

_____

_____

_____

_____

_____

_____

_____

Day 32

EVENING

Describe a series of mindful moments you incorporated into your day.

How did being present bring a sense of calm and awareness to a stress-free day?

_____

_____

_____

_____

_____

_____

_____

Day 32

Day 33

Dive into the
World of Fiction

MORNING

Engaging in reading can enhance brain and memory functions, alleviate stress, and induce a sense of relaxation.

As you get ready for your reading session tonight, please select a book or magazine. What is your choice, and what influenced your decision?

_____

_____

_____

_____

_____

_____

_____

Day 33

EVENING

Open the pages of the novel or indulge in the magazine.

Let the captivating stories and images transport you to a realm of imagination, offering a delightful escape from the stresses of the day.

Describe how it feels.

_____

_____

_____

_____

_____

_____

_____

Day 33

Day 34

Tea Time for Serenity

MORNING

Step away from your work and gift yourself a moment of tranquility.

Brew a soothing cup of tea (or coffee), allowing it's warmth to soothe your soul and create a gentle pause amidst your busy day.

How does this ignite your senses?

_____

_____

_____

_____

_____

_____

_____

_____

Day 34

EVENING

Tea contains caffeine, and when combined with l-theanine, it is believed to create a synergy that promotes mental clarity and concentration.

Did you experience instances of improved mental performance today following your tea consumption?

Write about your experience.

_____

_____

_____

_____

_____

_____

_____

Day 35

Breath Deeply,
Find Calm

MORNING

Focus on the simple rhythm of your breath – the inhale, the pause, the exhale.

Feel the oxygen infusing your body, calming your thoughts, and granting you a serene moment of stillness.

Describe this feeling?

_____

_____

_____

_____

_____

_____

_____

Day 35

EVENING

Engaging in breathwork exercises aids in alleviating bodily tension.

Have you noticed a reduction in workplace stress today as a result of concentrating on your breath?

Write about it.

_____

_____

_____

_____

_____

_____

_____

Day 35

Day 36

Hydrate Your Mind and Body

MORNING

Sip on cool, refreshing water to hydrate your body and mind.

With each sip, visualize stress melting away, replaced by a clear and focused state of being.

What are you releasing?

_____

_____

_____

_____

_____

_____

_____

Day 36

EVENING

Dehydration can trigger bodily stress leading to the release of stress hormones by the brain.

Write about how your body's stress level can rise when you're not properly hydrated, and explore the connection.

Day 36

Day 37

Creating Doodling
Delight

MORNING

Doodling is a creative outlet.

Find moments to use a pen and paper and allow your imagination to unfold.

In what ways do you think doodling can bring benefits to your well-being and mental clarity?

Day 37

EVENING

Doodling has therapeutic benefits and can help in bringing your thoughts together, clarifying ideas and maintaining focus.

How did doodling enhance your mental well-being and productivity today?

_____

_____

_____

_____

_____

_____

_____

Day 37

Day 38

Tune Into Relaxing Sounds

MORNING

Step away from your desk and immerse yourself in soothing music or calming sounds.

Let the melodies wash over you, offering a peace from the demands of work.

How does this contribute to your mental well-being?

_____

_____

_____

_____

_____

_____

_____

Day 38

EVENING

How has music influenced your mood
and perspective?

Reflect on your experiences with using
music as a tool for relaxation and stress
management today.

_____

_____

_____

_____

_____

_____

_____

Day 38

Day 39

Find Solace in Meditation

MORNING

Carve out a few minutes for meditation.

Close your eyes, inhale serenity, and exhale tension. Allow this mindful practice to create a serene sanctuary within the bustling day. Now, as you let go can you feel that tension melting away from different parts of your body? Write about it.

_____

_____

_____

_____

_____

_____

_____

Day 39

EVENING

Reflecting on your day, how did this mindfulness exercises impact your mental health and approach to workplace stress?

_____

_____

_____

_____

_____

_____

_____

Day 39

Day 40

Visualize Achieving
Your Goal

MORNING

What project or deadline do you have?

Close your eyes and picture yourself finishing that project, closing the deal, or meeting the deadline.

How does it look finished and complete? How does it feel achieving that accomplishment? How will you respond when you conquer this goal?

_____

_____

_____

_____

_____

_____

_____

Day 40

EVENING

How did visualizing achieving your goal improve productivity in your workplace?

Did you experience reduced stress and anxiety?

Write about it.

_____

_____

_____

_____

_____

_____

_____

Day 40

Day 41

Aromatherapy for the Soul

MORNING

Embrace the comfort of a relaxation spray or rollerball.

With each breath, let the familiar scent become a cue for mindful moments, instantly grounding and soothing.

Do you feel it easing your tension and anxiety?

Write about it.

_____

_____

_____

_____

_____

_____

_____

Day 41

EVENING

The essential oils used in this practice trigger messages to be sent to your brain's limbic system, which controls your emotions, memory and how you learn.

Reflect back on the day and write about how the aromatherapy helped your processing.

_____

_____

_____

_____

_____

_____

_____

Day 41

Day 42

Revisiting Intentions

MORNING

Reflecting on your journey so far, how do you plan to amplify your commitment to mental well-being and combat workplace stress in the days ahead?

_____

_____

_____

_____

_____

_____

_____

Day 42

EVENING

How did mapping out a plan for mental well-being and workplace stress improve your focus and clarity in the day?

_____

_____

_____

_____

_____

_____

_____

Day 42

Day 43

Gratitude in Everyday
Moments

MORNING

Describe a mundane activity and approach it with gratitude today.

What will the activity be?

What can you be grateful for?

_____

_____

_____

_____

_____

_____

_____

Day 43

EVENING

Reflecting on the mundane activity you approached with gratitude today, how did infusing gratitude into the ordinary enhance your sense of joy and appreciation?

_____

_____

_____

_____

_____

_____

_____

Day 43

Day 44

Creative Expression

MORNING

Creative expressions helps you to relax because they activate the parts of your brain that process emotions.

Share your creative expression for the day – a poem, a sketch, or any form of artistic outlet.

Write down or sketch out this expression.

_____

_____

_____

_____

_____

_____

_____

Day 44

EVENING

When you engaged in the calming activities, you triggered your body's relaxation response.

How did tapping into your creative side help you release stress at your workplace?

_____

_____

_____

_____

_____

_____

_____

Day 44

Day 45

Meditation Magic

MORNING

Five minutes of meditation a day could significantly reduce stress.

It can produce a deep state of relaxation and a tranquil mind.

How will you meditate today?

Day 45

EVENING

Reflect on the moments you meditated today.

How did it offer you clarity, resilience, and a sense of peace about your challenges at work?

_____

_____

_____

_____

_____

_____

_____

Day 45

Day 46

Culvating Resilience

MORNING

Resilience gives you the motivation to overcome stressors and be proactive if you see potential roadblocks.

What can you be resilient about today?

_____

_____

_____

_____

_____

_____

_____

Day 46

Write about your resilience in action.

How did you bounce back from a setback, and what strategies did you apply to maintain your peace?

_____

_____

_____

_____

_____

_____

_____

Day 47

Stress Management

MORNING

To help with your stress management, determine what causes your stress and notice your stress triggers.

Write them down and be specific.

_____

_____

_____

_____

_____

_____

_____

Day 47

EVENING

Journaling when you feel stressed will allow you to reflect and be mindful of how your body feels when you're overwhelmed.

How did noticing your stressors help with workplace stress?

_____

_____

_____

_____

_____

_____

_____

Day 47

Day 48

Nutrition Intentions

MORNING

Eating a healthy diet provides the energy needed to face those stress-filled moments.

What foods will you incorporate for healthy eating into your daily routine?

_____

_____

_____

_____

_____

_____

_____

Day 48

EVENING

Let's think more about eating healthy.

What foods make you feel truly alive and ready to conquer challenges.

What are they?

How does your body respond to this nourishment?

Write about it.

_____

_____

_____

_____

_____

_____

_____

Day 48

Day 49

Mindful Morning Delight

MORNING

Describe a nourishing breakfast that fuels your body and mind.

How will savoring each bite set a positive tone for the day ahead?

_____

_____

_____

_____

_____

_____

_____

Day 49

EVENING

Reflect on the experience of mindful eating.

How did slowing down and savoring each bite enhance your connection to your body's needs?

_____

_____

_____

_____

_____

_____

_____

Day 49

Day 50

Meditation Oasis

MORNING

Meditation can give you a sense of calm, peace and balance.

A few moments of stillness and mindfulness can create a sanctuary of calm within your busy day.

How will you meditate today?

_____

_____

_____

_____

_____

_____

_____

Day 50

EVENING

Meditation can help you perform
better at work.

How did it improve your ability
to multitask?

How has it impacted your
reactions to workplace stress
and your overall sense of calm?

_____

_____

_____

_____

_____

_____

_____

Day 50

Day 51

Energizing Movement

MORNING

Exercising is effective at reducing fatigue, improving alertness and concentration.

Share an exercise routine for the day.

_____

_____

_____

_____

_____

_____

_____

Day 51

EVENING

Take a moment to reflect on today's exercise.

How did it work its wonders?

Did you feel the fatigue melting away?

Did your mind light up with newfound clarity?

_____

_____

_____

_____

_____

_____

_____

Day 51

Day 52

Meditation Milestone

MORNING

Continue to practice
meditation this morning.

List ways it will improve your
focus and clarity at work.

_____

_____

_____

_____

_____

_____

_____

· EVENING

Reflect on your journey with meditation so far.

How has it transformed your approach to work stress and helped you reclaim a sense of inner peace?

_____

_____

_____

_____

_____

_____

_____

Day 52

Day 53

Acts of Self-Love

MORNING

Make this a day of healthy eating,
meditation, and exercise.

Each of these acts of self-love contributes
to relieving stress and fostering a sense
of well-being.

Write about your experiences, sensations,
and emotions.

Day 53

EVENING

Write about your thoughts after a day of healthy eating, meditation, and exercise.

How did these practices shape your mood and perspective on work stress?

_____

_____

_____

_____

_____

_____

_____

Day 54

Joyful Movement

MORNING

Write about a form of exercise
that brings you joy.

Then do it.

_____

_____

_____

_____

_____

_____

_____

Day 54

EVENING

As you reflect on your physical activity, how did it become a source of liberation from stress and a boost to your well-being?

_____

_____

_____

_____

_____

_____

_____

Day 54

Day 55

Meditation Reflection

MORNING

Describe any shifts you've noticed in your meditation practice.

How has it impacted your reactions to workplace stress and your overall sense of calm?

Day 55

EVENING

Now, as you conclude this reflection, set your sights on tomorrow.

How will you carry forward this commitment to nurturing your mental health and navigating workplace stress?

Write down one specific action or practice you plan to embrace.

_____

_____

_____

_____

_____

_____

_____

Day 55

Day 56

Setting Boundaries for
Mental Wellbeing

MORNING

Think about boundaries at work.

How would they create a sense of balance and prevent burnout?

_____

_____

_____

_____

_____

_____

_____

Day 56

EVENING

Reflect on the boundaries you've established to protect your mental health at work.

Write about instances where enforcing boundaries led to positive outcomes to reduce workplace stress.

_____

_____

_____

_____

_____

_____

_____

Day 56

Day 57

Reflect on Daily
Moments

MORNING

Write about how acknowledging small victories and triumphs at work support your mental resilience.

_____

_____

_____

_____

_____

_____

_____

Day 57

EVENING

Share the small victories you experienced today, no matter how insignificant they may seem.

How did these moments of success contribute to your sense of accomplishment and well-being with the workplace challenges?

_____

_____

_____

_____

_____

_____

_____

Day 57

Day 58

Holistic Reflection and Celebration

MORNING

It's been 58 days!

Think about what has been your best coping mechanism to address burnout and workplace stress?

What is it?

_____

_____

_____

_____

_____

_____

_____

Day 58

EVENING

Celebrate your growth and
commit to continuing these
practices in the days to come.

How will you do this?

_____

_____

_____

_____

_____

_____

_____

Day 58

Day 59

Gratitude as a Stress-Busting Tool

MORNING

Write about three things you're grateful for in your work environment.

Dive into these emotions and how practicing gratitude shifts your perspective on workplace stress.

_____

_____

_____

_____

_____

_____

_____

Day 59

EVENING

Reflect on your day.

Describe moments when focusing on gratitude has alleviated stress and improved your mental state.

_____

_____

_____

_____

_____

_____

_____

Day 59

Day 60

Holistic Reflection and Celebration

MORNING

Congratulations on completing this remarkable 60-day journey towards nurturing your mental well-being and conquering workplace stress!

Write about how this journey has shaped your mindset, empowered your actions, and laid the foundation for a life of balance and joy.

Day 60

EVENING

Remember that your journey of self-care and mental health is ongoing.

Now, visualize yourself stepping into the next day with intention and determination. Keep a journal close, continue writing in times of stress and challenge.

How do you feel about this accomplishment?

_____

_____

_____

_____

_____

_____

_____

Day 60

Make self-care a priority not an option!